This Workbook Belongs To: _____

STEPS

to Healthy Touching

SECOND EDITION

Activities to Help Kids Understand and Control Their Problems with Touching

These materials are designed for children ages five through twelve and developmentally delayed adolescents who exhibit sexually abusive behavior toward other children–particularly for abuse-reactive children who have been sexually victimized themselves.

Kee MacFarlane, M.S.W.

Carolyn Cunningham, Ph.D.

KIDSRIGHTS®

Steps to Healthy Touching, Second Edition
Activities to Help Kids Understand and Control Their Problems with Touching

© 2003 by Kee MacFarlane and Carolyn Cunningham—text
© 2003 by KIDSRIGHTS—illustration

Published by KIDSRIGHTS®, an imprint of JIST Publishing, Inc.

8902 Otis Avenue
Indianapolis, IN 46216-1033
Phone: 800-892-5437
Toll-free fax: 877-543-7001
E-mail: kidsrights@jist.com
Web site: www.kidsrights.com

A Note to Counselors and Other Helping Professionals Using This Book

Children abusing other children. The materials in this activity book are of a sensitive nature and should be used by a trained professional as one part of a more comprehensive program. Many children who act out inappropriately have themselves been sexually abused or observed abuse, and this situation will often require the services of an experienced therapist. A separate counselor's/teacher's guide detailed below is available from the publisher to help you use this activity book. But please note that this activity book is not to be considered as a solution to a serious problem, only as a tool to assist the therapeutic process provided by an experienced and trained professional. Also, as you probably know, it is your legal responsibility to immediately report any suspected or known situations of child abuse to the appropriate police or child welfare authority. It is an unfortunate reality, but our highest level of responsibility is to protect children from abuse or potential abuse. We wish you well and hope that this material helps in some small way.

A separate counselor's/teacher's guide (ISBN 1-55864-139-4) supports this workbook and is available from KIDSRIGHTS. The guide offers information on using the workbook as part of your comprehensive treatment. Call 1-800-892-5437 for details.

Quantity discounts are available for KIDSRIGHTS products. Also, many KIDSRIGHTS products are available in Spanish. For a list of products and our free catalog, call 1-800-892-5437 or visit www.kidsrights.com.

Copy Editors: Tara Morrall, Sandy Cameron
Cover and Interior Designer: Aleata Howard
Proofreader: Jeanne Clark

Printed in the United States of America

07 06 05 04 03   9 8 7 6 5 4 3 2 1

We have been careful to provide accurate information throughout this book, but it is possible that errors have been introduced. Please consider this in making any important decisions. Trust your own judgment above all else and in all things.

ISBN 1-55864-138-6

Contents

Dedication

This workbook is dedicated to the first group of children, parents, and therapists in the Support Program for Abusive-Reactive Kids (SPARK), who taught one another about this difficult problem and who struggled together to find a process for treating it, and to the memory of Faye Honey Knopp, a pioneer and supporter in the treatment of young offenders.

Introduction

Everyone usually has one or two big problems that they need help with. This workbook was made to help you with your problem of touching other kids in ways that are wrong or hurtful. It can also help you with the problem of showing your private parts to kids who don't want to see them. This is a workbook about stuff that most people don't want to talk about: problems with sexual behavior.

Twelve Steps

There are twelve steps to follow and learn. You can think of this workbook as kind of a football game that you really need to win. Each step has tasks for you to do, questions for you to answer, and things for you to think about. At the end of every step you will gain yards toward your touchdown. When you're all done with the workbook, you'll have gained 100 yards and scored a touchdown. Some of the steps are worth more yards than others because some are harder than others. Some steps are going to take longer than others to finish, and sometimes you might forget things you learned in a previous step and have to go back and try again. That's okay. This is not a race. It is a group of steps that can help you learn about yourself, your feelings, and your problem with touching.

Homework

Now there *is* one part you might not like—homework. (Yuck—homework!) Yes, there is some work for you to do at home, but it isn't the kind of hard or boring homework you sometimes get at school. It's more like a bunch of little projects to figure out, and it won't take you very long to do them. But you will have to get them signed by one of your parents or a grown-up that you live with before you hand them in. If you don't, you won't be able to go on to the next step. It helps to have some grown-ups on your team, anyway, because you're going to need some help to beat this touching problem. Every team needs many players, and even the best player can't win a football game by himself!

Your Goal

Each time you finish a step, you will be working to make your touching problem go down. That's why the goal is to get a touchdown! When you finish the twelfth step, you will have reached your goal of learning to control your problem of touching other people in hurtful ways. A true touchdown! It takes a lot of work to control a big problem, but reaching the goal will make you stronger and healthier. Remember, many people are on your team and are cheering for you, so give it your best.

12
STEPS FOR KIDS
who have problems with touching

1. I have a problem with touching that is too tough for me to handle by myself. It is bigger than I am.

2. I believe that there are people who care about me who can help me with my touching problem. I believe that God will help me too, if I ask.

3. I am making up my mind to let people who know and understand this problem help me to get power over it.

4. I have decided to stop blaming other people or events for everything and to admit how big my problem really is.

5. I admit to myself, to other people, and to God exactly what I have done that is wrong and harmful to others.

6. I am ready to give up my problem (even though sometimes the touching feels good) and find another way to show my feelings.

7. I am learning that there are some things about myself that I can change and other things that I cannot change. I am working on changing the things I can.

8. I accept that I cannot change other people or their behavior. They are the only ones who can change themselves—and only if they want to. This includes my parents, other grown-ups, and my friends.

9. I am learning to recognize the times when I need help from others, including God, and I am willing to ask for help because I need it.

10. I have made a list of everyone I have hurt by my behavior (including myself), and I will try to make up, in any way I can, for the harm I have caused.

11. I continue to think about my problem, and I am willing to ask for help if I feel it coming back.

12. I will help other kids who have this problem by sharing my own problem and feelings and by helping them to see that it is too tough for them to handle by themselves.

Alternative
12
STEPS FOR KIDS
who have problems with touching

1. I have a problem with touching that is too tough for me to handle by myself. It is bigger than I am.

2. I believe that there are people who care about me who can help me with my touching problem.

3. I am making up my mind to let people who know and understand this problem help me to get power over it.

4. I have decided to stop blaming other people or events for everything and to admit how big my problem really is.

5. I admit to myself and to other people exactly what I have done that is wrong and harmful to others.

6. I am ready to give up my problem (even though sometimes the touching feels good) and find another way to show my feelings.

7. I am learning that there are some things about myself that I can change and other things that I cannot change. I am working on changing the things I can.

8. I accept that I cannot change other people or their behavior. They are the only ones who can change themselves—and only if they want to. This includes my parents, other grown-ups, and my friends.

9. I am learning to recognize the times when I need help from others, and I am willing to ask for help because I need it.

10. I have made a list of everyone I have hurt by my behavior (including myself), and I will try to make up, in any way I can, for the harm I have caused.

11. I continue to think about my problem, and I am willing to ask for help if I feel it coming back.

12. I will help other kids who have this problem by sharing my own problem and feelings and by helping them to see that it is too tough for them to handle by themselves.

"I have a problem with touching that is too tough for me to handle by myself. It is bigger than I am."

STEP

1

Read Step 1 out loud two times slowly.

Feelings
I Have When I
Admit That I Have
a Problem

Step 1 is one of the hardest and most important steps.

Lots of kids feel embarrassed, ashamed, or scared inside when they have to talk about their problems with touching. They do all kinds of things to avoid talking about it. They clown around, blame others, change the subject, act really angry, or talk nonstop about other subjects. Some people call these things defenses or masks. Some kids use defenses to hide their problems the way a mask hides your face.

How do you *really* feel when you start to admit to yourself that you have a big problem? Draw or write the feelings on this page.

Masking Your Feelings

On Halloween, we wear real masks to hide our faces. But sometimes we wear "imaginary masks"—the kind that other people can't see. Imaginary masks hide our feelings from other people. You are wearing an imaginary mask when you're pretending to feel something that you don't really feel.

Examples of imaginary masks are
- ▼ Acting like everything is fine when it isn't
- ▼ Saying you don't care about something when you do
- ▼ Pretending to be super nice when you're really angry inside
- ▼ Acting angry when what you really feel is hurt

What masks do you wear that keep you from admitting to yourself that you have a problem with touching? On this page or another piece of paper draw the mask or masks that you wear to hide your feelings.

You and your group can make "feelings masks" out of paper plates. For example, clown, grouch, people pleaser, sad sack, or the "who-cares kid." Give the masks to each other to wear when you are acting like you are feeling certain things.

Picture yourself taking off the masks. Draw a picture of yourself without any masks, saying to yourself, "I have a touching problem that is too tough for me to handle by myself. It is bigger than I am."

Draw your problem right next to the picture of you. How much bigger is it than you?

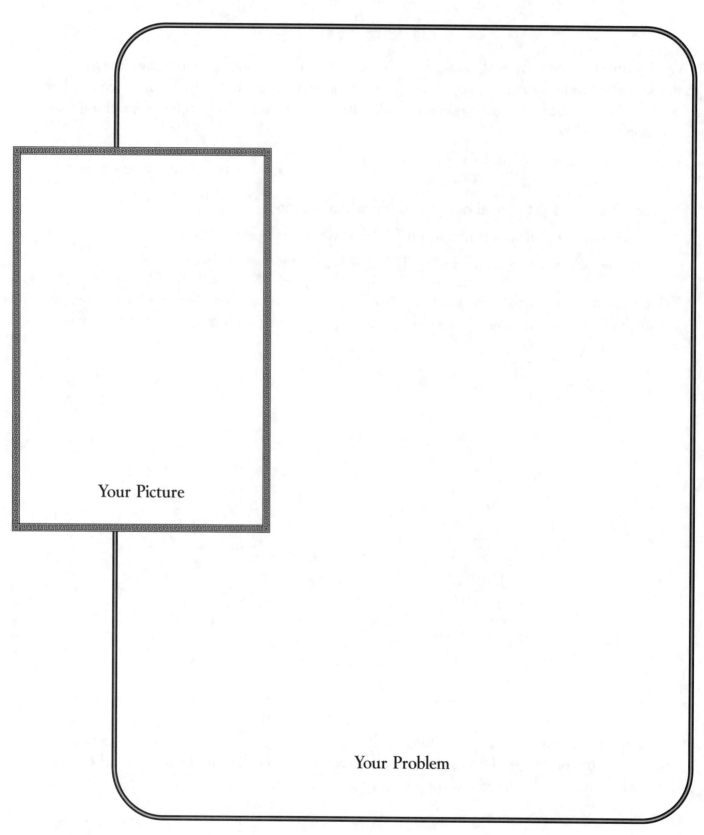

Your Picture

Your Problem

Step 1
Homework
Assignment

Once a day for the next week, remind yourself that you have a problem that is bigger than you are. It will help you to remember if you do it at the same time every day—like while you brush your teeth or take a bath. Just pause for a minute and say, "I have a touching problem that is too tough for me to handle by myself. It is bigger than I am."

Also, pay attention to any times when you are pretending to feel things that you don't really feel or when you are hiding your real feelings. If you catch yourself putting on an "imaginary mask," stop and think about what you are *really* feeling. Then go and tell someone what it is.

_____   _____
(Parent/Caretaker Signature)   (Date)

The Step that I learned last week said (write down your answer or have someone else write it for you) _____

_____

_____

_____

_____

I practiced what I learned last week by _____

_____

_____

_____

STEP
1

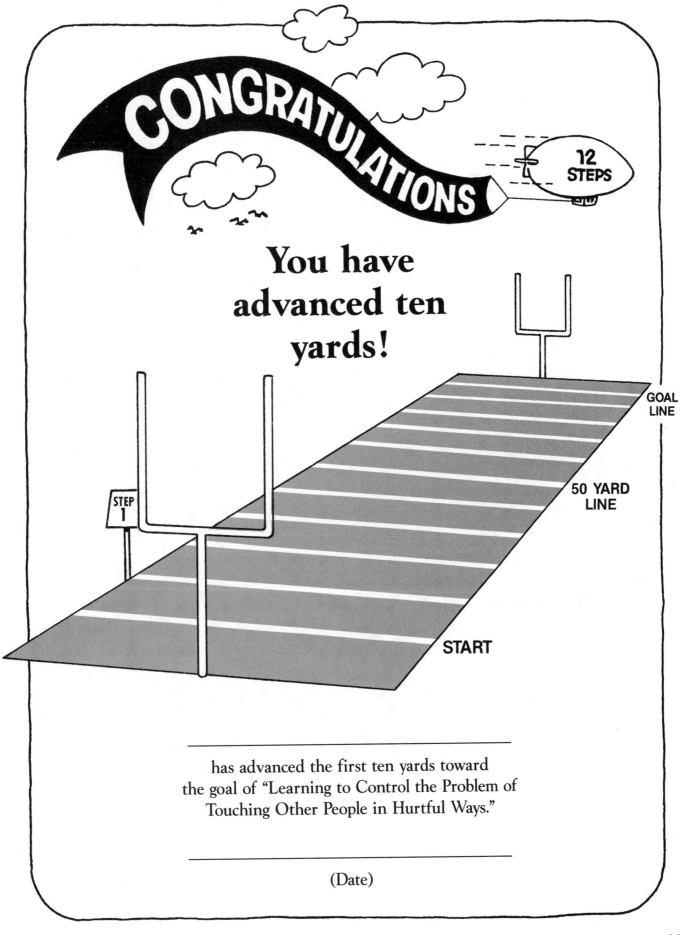

CONGRATULATIONS

12 STEPS

You have advanced ten yards!

GOAL LINE

50 YARD LINE

STEP 1

START

_____

has advanced the first ten yards toward
the goal of "Learning to Control the Problem of
Touching Other People in Hurtful Ways."

_____

(Date)

"I believe that there are people who care about me who can help me with my problem. I believe that God will help me too, if I ask."

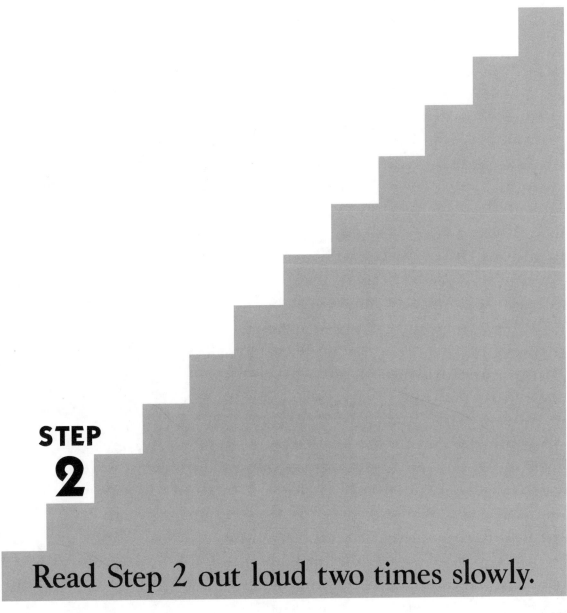

STEP 2

Read Step 2 out loud two times slowly.

"I believe that there are people who care about me who can help me with my problem."

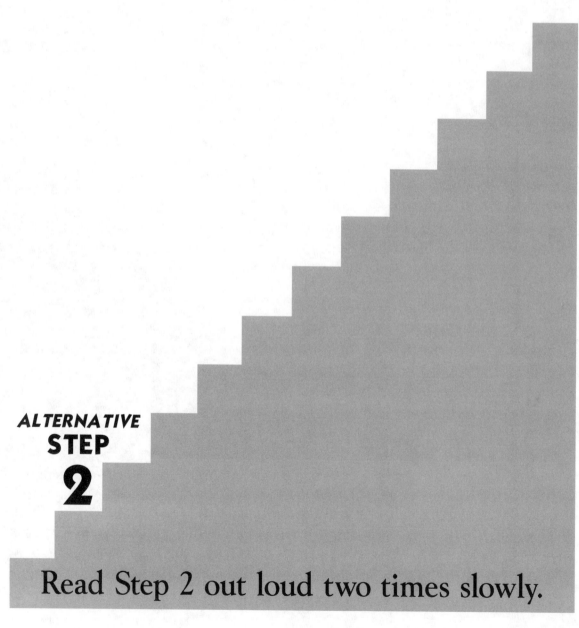

ALTERNATIVE
STEP
2

Read Step 2 out loud two times slowly.

People Who Care About Me

Lots of people care about you. How do you know when people care about you?

Draw a picture or make a list of the special people in your life who care about you. Write their names next to their pictures. Put a check mark next to the people who you will let help you with your problem. Talk about the ways that these special people might be able to help you.

This is _____

This is _____

This is _____

This is _____

This is _____

God Cares About Me

(Optional Exercise)

People have different ideas about what God looks like. Some people don't have any picture of God in their minds, but they do believe that there is a "higher power" that is more powerful than they are. Your "higher power" could even be a person or people that you know. It could be a group you're in, or it could be something less real–like a rainbow or the sky. A "higher power" gives you help and strength...the feeling that you're cared for.

Draw a picture of the way you see God or your higher power. Then draw yourself next to your God or higher power and think about the help you are getting. Think about being cared for and protected by your higher power. Guess what? You are!

Step 2
Homework
Assignment

Pick one or more of the special people in your life and ask them to help you with something this week. It's better if you ask for help with a feelings problem or something that is bothering you instead of with something ordinary like your math homework. Maybe they can help you understand your feelings about something or someone—maybe they once felt that way.

See if it's hard for you to ask for help and how it felt after you did it. Practice doing it whenever you can.

The feeling or problem that I needed help with: _____

_____

_____

_____

_____

The person who helped me: _____

_____

_____

_____

_____

_____   _____
(Parent/Caretaker Signature)   (Date)

The Step that I learned last week said (write down your answer or have someone else write it for you) _____

_____

_____

_____

_____

I practiced what I learned last week by _____

_____

_____

_____

_____

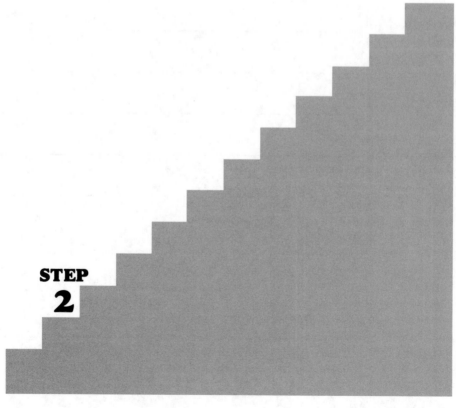

STEP
2

CONGRATULATIONS

12 STEPS

You have advanced five more yards!

STEP 2

GOAL LINE

50 YARD LINE

START

_____

has advanced five more yards toward
the goal of "Learning to Control the Problem of
Touching Other People in Hurtful Ways."

_____

(Date)

"I am making up my mind to let people who know and understand this problem help me to get power over it."

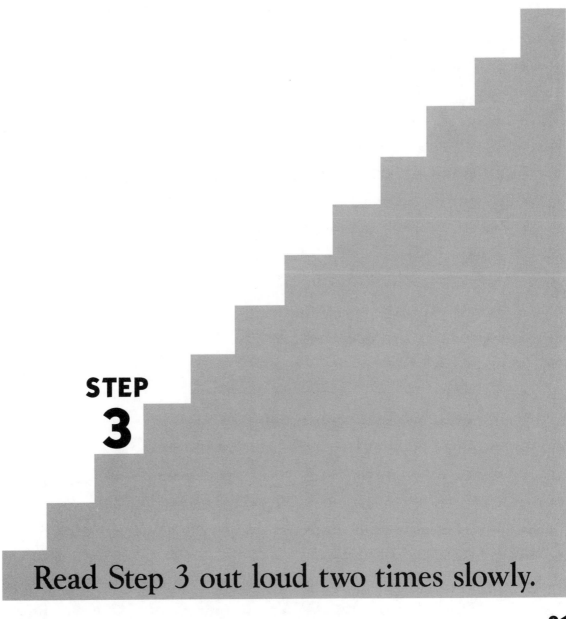

STEP
3

Read Step 3 out loud two times slowly.

Asking
for Help

Some kids feel that it is babyish to need help or to ask for help. It's really not babyish at all to ask for help. You are growing up when you begin to learn that there are some things you can do all by yourself and some things or problems with which you need help. People who have problems that are bigger than they are *always* need to ask for help.

Think about the people who know about your problem with touching. Draw a picture that shows them helping you.

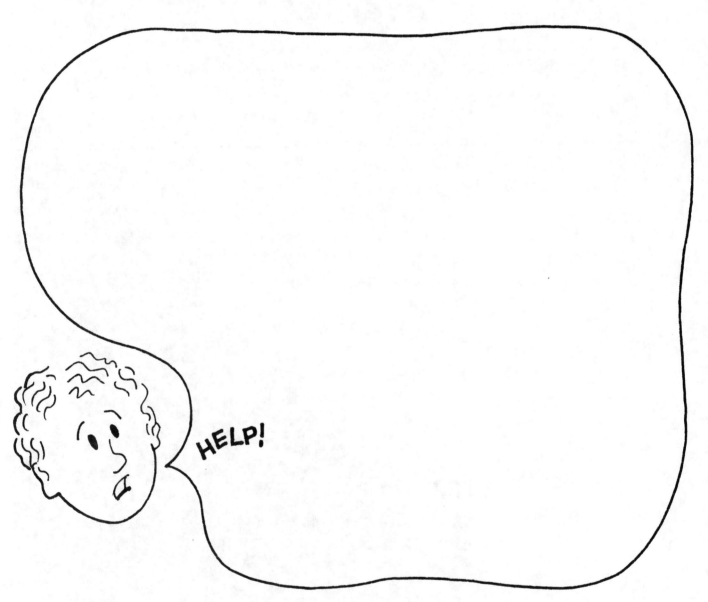

How do you feel about telling someone more about your problem? How do you feel about letting someone help you with it?

Step 3
Homework
Assignment

This week, talk with someone about your problem with touching. It can be someone who already knows about it, like one of your parents or another member of your family, but tell them something more than they already know. Don't try to act like your problem is no big deal or like you already have control over it. Tell them that your problem is too tough for you to handle by yourself and ask for their help. Figure out together some of the ways that they might help (like being there to listen or to help you in case the urge to touch comes back).

Try to find at least three ways that person, or one way three people, can help you with your touching problem. Write down the ways and get either one, two, or three people to sign their initials showing that they agree to help you.

The Helping Contract

I recognize that _____ has a problem with touching, and I agree to help him/her get better control over it in the following way(s):

1. _____

    _____

    _____   _____
                                                                                          (Initials)

2. _____

    _____

    _____   _____
                                                                                          (Initials)

3. _____

    _____

    _____   _____
                                                                                          (Initials)

_____   _____
(Parent/Caretaker Signature)   (Date)

The Step that I learned last week said (write down your answer or have someone else write it for you) _____

_____

_____

_____

_____

I practiced what I learned last week by _____

_____

_____

_____

_____

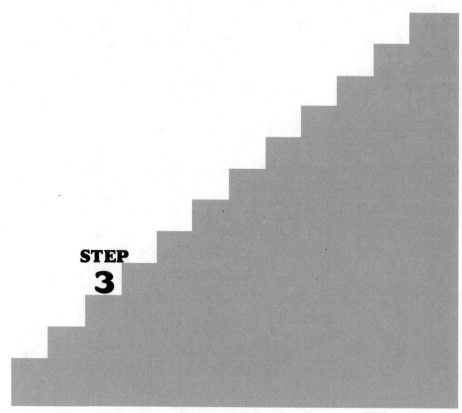

STEP
3

CONGRATULATIONS

12 STEPS

You have advanced five more yards!

GOAL LINE

STEP 3

50 YARD LINE

START

YOU HAVE NOW COMPLETED 3 STEPS!

_____

has advanced five more yards toward
the goal of "Learning to Control the Problem of
Touching Other People in Hurtful Ways."

_____

(Date)

"I have decided to stop blaming other people or events for everything and to admit how big my problem really is."

STEP 4

Read Step 4 out loud two times slowly.

Me & My
Blaming Mask

Blaming is a mask many people wear when they feel too afraid to face or admit that they have a problem. Some kids blame the person they touched by saying, "He made me do it" or "She liked it." Some kids blame their parents by saying, "My mom made me mad...that's why I did it." Some kids blame everyone for everything.

Make a picture of you taking off your blaming mask.

My
Blaming
List

On this page, make a list of the people you blamed for your touching problem and what part of it you blamed them for causing.

People I have blamed:

1._____

_____

_____

_____

2._____

_____

_____

_____

3._____

_____

_____

_____

4._____

_____

_____

What I blamed them for:

1._____

_____

_____

_____

2._____

_____

_____

_____

3._____

_____

_____

_____

4._____

_____

_____

My Stop Sign

Make a stop sign* that says "Stop and Think."

This is a reminder that you must stop blaming other people for your problem with touching. You might want to put your stop sign up in your room at home to remind yourself to "Stop and Think."

NO MORE BLAMING

I CAN HANDLE IT

FACE UP TO IT

STOP AND THINK

TAKE RESPONSIBILITY

BLAMING STINKS

IT'S LAME TO BLAME

BLAMING IS FOR LOSERS

BLAMING IS KIDS' STUFF

* Cardboard and craft sticks work well.

Step 4
Homework
Assignment

Weekly Blaming List

Make a list of the times during the week you caught yourself blaming others for things that you did.

I blamed or started to blame (person's name)	**For**
1._____	1._____
_____	_____
_____	_____
2._____	2._____
_____	_____
_____	_____
3._____	3._____
_____	_____
_____	_____
4._____	4._____
_____	_____
_____	_____

_____   _____

(Parent/Caretaker Signature)   (Date)

The Step that I learned last week said (write down your answer or have someone else write it for you) _____

_____

_____

_____

_____

I practiced what I learned last week by _____

_____

_____

_____

_____

STEP 4

CONGRATULATIONS

12 STEPS

You have advanced ten more yards!

STEP 4

GOAL LINE

50 YARD LINE

START

_____

has advanced ten more yards toward
the goal of "Learning to Control the Problem of
Touching Other People in Hurtful Ways."

_____

(Date)

"I admit to myself, to other people, and to God exactly what I have done that is wrong and harmful to others."

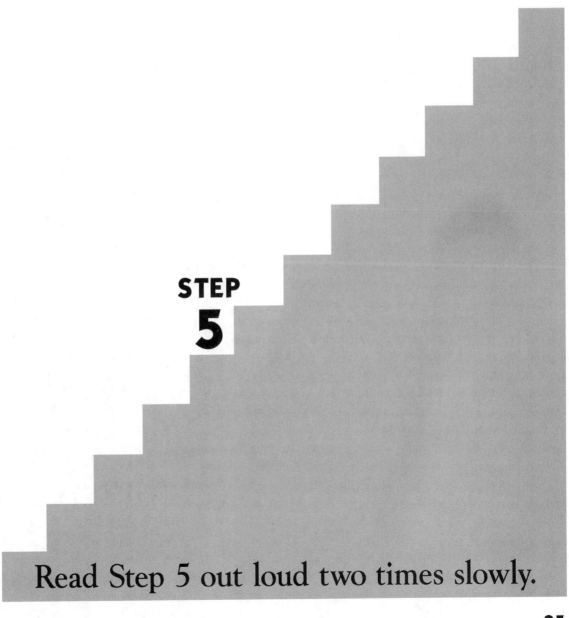

STEP
5

Read Step 5 out loud two times slowly.

"I admit to myself and to other people exactly what I have done that is wrong and harmful to others."

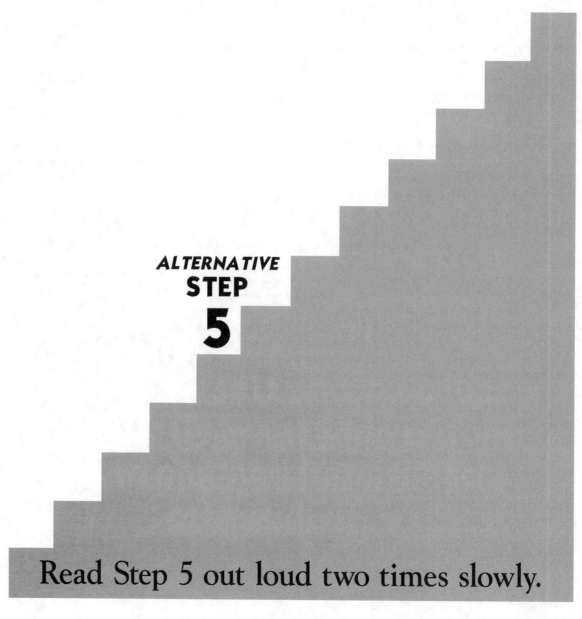

ALTERNATIVE
STEP
5

Read Step 5 out loud two times slowly.

What Was Going on Inside of Me Before I Was Hurtful

Now it's time to remember and write down what you said and what you thought about just *before* you touched someone else in a way that was wrong.

Before I Touched

1. I was thinking _____

_____

_____

_____

2. I was feeling _____

_____

_____

_____

3. I said _____

_____

_____

_____

4. I was doing _____

_____

_____

_____

What Is a Victim?

A victim is a person who is harmed by someone or something. A person who is a victim doesn't always show it and, sometimes, they don't even know it until later. Victims have had something wrong or bad happen to them that wasn't their fault.

Put a check mark next to the reasons that go with what you did.

The person or people I touched are victims because of one or more of the following reasons:

1. _____ They were younger or smaller than I was.

2. _____ They didn't want to be touched in that way.

3. _____ I forced them or told them they had to do things they didn't want to do.

4. _____ I tricked them into doing something.

5. _____ They didn't know it was wrong.

6. _____ They were too young or too scared to say no and run away.

7. _____ I told them not to tell.

8. _____ Even if they agreed to it, or started it, or acted like they liked it, they didn't know what would happen later or how they would feel afterward.

9. _____ I knew that it was wrong.

Can you think of any other reasons?

Do you understand why your victim is not being blamed for what happened?

Do you still feel like it was mostly the victim's fault? Why?

Talk about those feelings.

If you were a victim of someone or something when you were younger, which of the nine reasons above made you a victim?

_____

Who I Touched

It is important to remember, think about, and talk about the person or people who you victimized, hurt, or touched in a way that was wrong. Close your eyes and picture that person or people in your mind. Then, fill in this page. (Use a separate page for each victim.)

The person I victimized is a   girl   boy   (circle one)

He/She was _____ years old when it happened.

I had known him/her for _____. (length of time)

His/Her name is _____.

Draw a picture of that person below.

Think about why you picked that person to victimize, and then talk about your reasons.

_____

_____

Who I Touched

It is important to remember, think about, and talk about the person or people who you victimized, hurt, or touched in a way that was wrong. Close your eyes and picture that person or people in your mind. Then, fill in this page. (Use a separate page for each victim.)

The person I victimized is a   girl   boy   (circle one)

He/She was _____ years old when it happened.

I had known him/her for _____. (length of time)

His/Her name is _____.

Draw a picture of that person below.

Think about why you picked that person to victimize, and then talk about your reasons.

_____

_____

Step 5
Homework
Assignment
Part I

Putting Yourself in Someone Else's Shoes

For one day next week, try to see what someone else's life is like by living for a while like they live or pretending to be them. This is called "putting yourself in someone else's shoes." For example, if you choose your younger brothers or sisters, try eating what they eat, doing their chores, watching their favorite T.V. shows, or helping them with their homework. You might choose someone who is very old—someone who walks and talks slowly and forgets things. You might choose someone who has a disability—for example, someone who walks with a limp or a crutch or a cane; someone who is deaf (try cotton in your ears and write down everything you want to say on a pad of paper); or someone who is blind. If you decide to cover your eyes to see what being blind is like, always have someone walk beside you to make sure you don't hurt yourself.

_____   _____
(Parent/Caretaker Signature)   (Date)

What I Did

It is also important to remember *exactly* what you did to the other person or people. It is hard to think about things that you don't want to remember, but it is important to do if you are going to change.

What Happened

What I did:

1. First I _____

_____

_____

2. Then _____

_____

_____

3. Then _____

_____

_____

4. Then _____

_____

_____

What the other kid did:

1. First he/she _____

_____

_____

2. Then _____

_____

_____

3. Then _____

_____

_____

4. Then _____

_____

_____

Part of remembering what you did is being able to picture it in your mind. You would probably rather block it out of your mind, but that won't make it go away. In your mind, picture what you did and then draw it on this page. It's hard to do, but try.

43

If anything like this ever happened to you when you were younger, try to draw what that looked like. Tell somebody about it. Then talk about how it made you feel.

44

Thoughts and Feelings During the Touching

Think back to when you were touching the other person. Where were you? Who else was there? Try to remember what you said and what you were thinking at the time. Think about what the other person said when you were doing the touching. How do you think he or she was feeling?

While I Was Touching

Me:

1. I said _____

_____

_____

2. I was thinking _____

_____

_____

3. I was feeling _____

_____

_____

_____

The Other Kid:

1. He/She said _____

_____

_____

2. He/She might have been thinking ____

_____

_____

3. He/She probably was feeling _____

_____

_____

_____

Being and Doing

Who you are and what you did are two different things. You are not a bad person just because you did a bad thing. Lots of good people sometimes do bad things. But they learn from their mistakes and they learn how to change their behavior. People who care about you don't like what you did, but they still like *you*. It is important that *you* still like you, too.

On page 43, you drew a picture of what you did. On this page draw a picture of you.

See the difference between you and what you did? Which picture do you like better? Which one is the you that you want to be?

46

After
the Touching

Now that you've remembered and talked about the touching you did, think about what happened afterward—how you were feeling, what you and the other kid said or did. Remember what you felt and thought *before* you got caught.

What Happened Afterward

Me:

1. I said _____

_____

_____

2. What I did _____

_____

_____

3. I thought about _____

_____

_____

_____

4. I was feeling _____

_____

_____

The Other Kid:

1. He/She said _____

_____

_____

2. What he/she did _____

_____

_____

3. He/She might have thought _____

_____

_____

4. He/She probably felt _____

_____

_____

This has been the longest and hardest step of all. That's why you earn twice as many yards for this step as you do for any other step! You're learning that it takes a lot of hard work to control the problem of touching other people in hurtful ways. Being able to talk about your problem and your feelings is what this step is all about. How are you feeling now that you've finished this step? Write down or draw a picture of how you are feeling.

I am feeling _____

_____

_____

Step 5
Homework
Assignment
Part II

Admitting Mistakes

By the time most people grow up, they have made a few bad mistakes that they had to admit later. This week, find a grown-up who made a mistake and admitted it. Ask him or her to tell you all about it. For example, what was the mistake? How did it happen? Who was it admitted to? What made him or her admit it? How did he or she feel at the time? How does he or she feel now?

On this page, either you or the grown-up should write down what the mistake was and who it was admitted to. Next week come back and describe it with the details. Try to remember the answers to all of the questions on this page.

The person who made the mistake was _____

The mistake that he/she made was _____

_____

_____

_____

The person or people it was admitted to was/were _____

_____

_____

_____   _____
(Parent/Caretaker Signature)   (Date)

The Step that I learned last week said (write down your answer or have someone else write it for you) _____

_____

_____

_____

_____

I practiced what I learned last week by _____

_____

_____

_____

_____

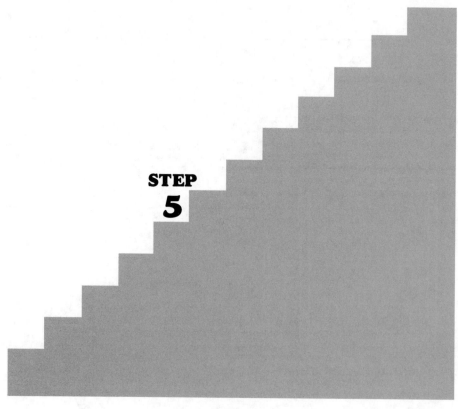

STEP
5

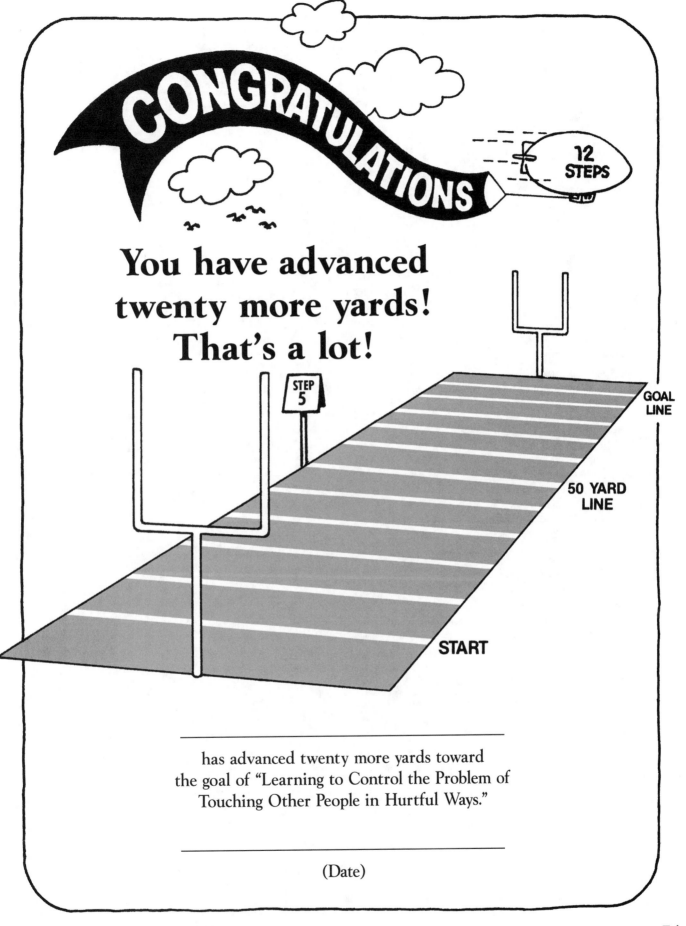

CONGRATULATIONS

12 STEPS

You have advanced
twenty more yards!
That's a lot!

STEP 5

GOAL LINE

50 YARD LINE

START

_____

has advanced twenty more yards toward
the goal of "Learning to Control the Problem of
Touching Other People in Hurtful Ways."

_____

(Date)

"I am ready to give up my problem (even though sometimes the touching feels good) and find another way to show my feelings."

STEP 6

Read Step 6 out loud two times slowly.

Draw a picture of you putting your problem, along with the masks that you used to wear, into a balloon. Draw a picture of the balloon sailing off.

Self-Talk

It is time to learn some new ways to deal with painful feelings—ways that have nothing to do with touching. Along with talking to other people about your feelings, you can also talk yourself into feeling better. This is called "self-talk." It takes practice, but if you get good at it, it can help you to handle scary or painful feelings.

These are some examples of self-talk that you can use:

"You have to have rain in order to get a rainbow."

"I'm mad, but I *can* control my anger."

"Everybody makes mistakes. I'll do better next time."

"Everybody is scared sometimes."

"It's okay to be sad. I have a good reason."

"I may not be perfect, but I'm special because I'm me."

"I might meet a new friend soon."

"Everyone has bad days—this is one of mine."

"Don't sweat the small stuff."

"I'll be okay tomorrow."

"There are lots of people who care about me."

"Chill out, cool it, hang in there."

Try making up some self-talk of your own. Practice self-talk this week whenever you are feeling upset.

Letting Your Feelings Show

What is the hardest feeling for you to express or show to other people? For example, is it hurt feelings, anger, fear, or some other feeling? What feeling do you most often stuff down inside of yourself? Think about it for a few minutes, and then fill in the answer.

The feeling that is hardest for me to show is _____

Think about what you usually do when you are feeling this way. If you show this feeling at all, how do you show it to other people?

The way I act when I feel this way is _____

_____

If you don't show this feeling very much or you act in a way that is different from how you really feel, how do you know that you are feeling it? Think about the signs that tell you what you're feeling, and then fill in the answer.

I know I'm feeling _____ because _____

_____

Now think about a way (or a better way) to show the feeling that is hardest for you to show. How could you show it so that other people can understand and help you with it?

I could show my _____ feeling by _____

_____

The next time you are feeling that way, try out your new way of showing it, with someone you know. Then come back and tell how it worked.

Step 6
Homework
Assignment

Feelings Chart

This week, keep track of the ways you let people know how you are feeling.

Feelings I had during the week:

1._____

_____

_____

2._____

_____

_____

3._____

_____

_____

4._____

_____

_____

The way that I let people know:

1._____

_____

_____

2._____

_____

_____

3._____

_____

_____

4._____

_____

_____

_____
(Parent/Caretaker Signature)

_____
(Date)

The Step that I learned last week said (write down your answer or have someone else write it for you) _____

_____

_____

_____

_____

I practiced what I learned last week by _____

_____

_____

_____

_____

STEP
6

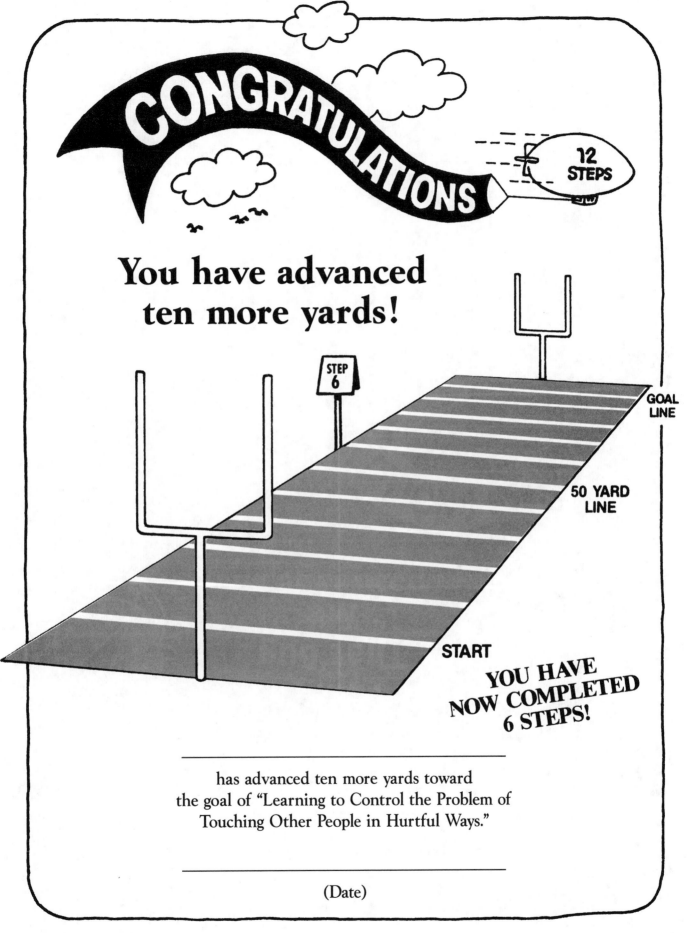

CONGRATULATIONS

12 STEPS

You have advanced
ten more yards!

STEP 6

GOAL LINE

50 YARD LINE

START

YOU HAVE NOW COMPLETED 6 STEPS!

_____

has advanced ten more yards toward
the goal of "Learning to Control the Problem of
Touching Other People in Hurtful Ways."

_____

(Date)

"I am learning that there are some things about myself that I can change and other things that I cannot change. I am working on changing the things I can."

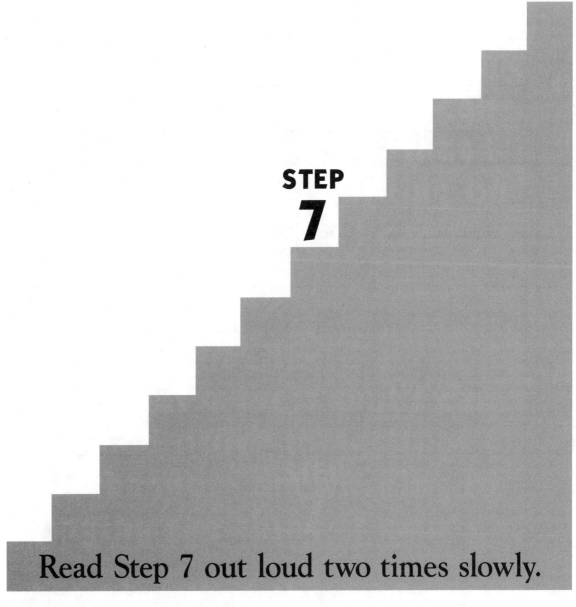

STEP
7

Read Step 7 out loud two times slowly.

Things I Wish I Could Change

Each and every one of us has things about ourselves that we don't like and wish we could change. Those things usually have to do with the way we look (appearance), the way we act (behavior), the way we do things (performance), or the way we feel inside (emotions).

Make a list of the things about yourself that you don't like and want to change.

Things about my appearance that I wish I could change:

1. _____

2. _____

3. _____

4. _____

Things about my behavior that I wish I could change:

1. _____

2. _____

3. _____

4. _____

Things that I don't do very well that I wish I could change:

1. _____

2. _____

3. _____

4. _____

Feelings that I don't like having that I wish I could change:

1. _____

2. _____

3. _____

4. _____

Things
I Cannot
Change

There are some things about ourselves that we can change (like the way we act in certain situations) and some things about ourselves that we cannot change (like the color of our eyes or certain feelings).

Look carefully at the list you just made. What are the things on your list about yourself that you can change? What are the things on your list that you cannot change?

Put the things you can change about yourself on one side of the paper and the things you cannot change about yourself on the other side.

Things on my list that I CAN change:

1. _____

   _____

   _____

2. _____

   _____

   _____

3. _____

   _____

   _____

4. _____

   _____

   _____

Things on my list that I CANNOT change:

1. _____

   _____

   _____

2. _____

   _____

   _____

3. _____

   _____

   _____

4. _____

   _____

   _____

My Plan for Change

For each thing about yourself that you *can* change, make a plan and decide how and what you can do to make that change. You may need someone to help you make your plan. Who will it be?

These are things I CAN change about myself:

1. _____

2. _____

3. _____

This is how I am going to change:

1. _____

2. _____

3. _____

These people can help me:

1. _____

2. _____

3. _____

The Critic
Inside You

Sometimes we spend a lot of time thinking about the things that we cannot change about ourselves. We have a voice inside ourselves that always reminds us about these things that we cannot change. Some people call this voice their "critic" because it criticizes them and puts them down. Someone's critic might say, "Your hair is ugly" or "You're dumb" or "You're not good enough." Do you have a name for the critical voice inside of you?

You can picture your critic as looking like a big vulture who stands over you saying negative things to you. What does your vulture say to you that makes you feel bad? Write some of those things inside the vulture's voice balloons.

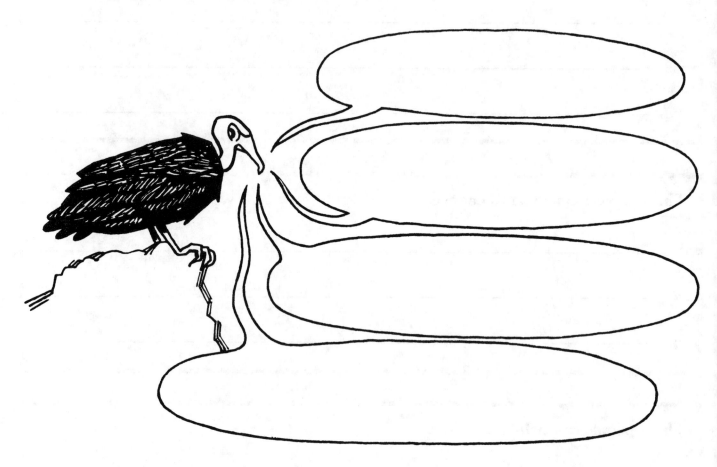

You need to learn to keep the vulture quiet by saying "Stop!" to that voice inside of you. You can answer it back by saying "That's not true!" Remember, it's *your* vulture because it's really just *you* criticizing yourself. That's why it appears when you're feeling bad about yourself. You have created it; you can make it go away. Try stopping your vulture this week.

Things
I Wouldn't
Change

Now that you are learning to talk to the critical vulture who says negative things about you, let's look at the things about you that are special—the things you like about yourself. Make a list of the good things about you that you want to keep.

Things about my appearance that I like:

1. _____

2. _____

3. _____

4. _____

Turn the page for more...

Things that I do well:

1. _____
2. _____
3. _____
4. _____

Good behaviors or feelings that I have:

1. _____
2. _____
3. _____
4. _____

Nice things that other people say about me:

1. _____
2. _____
3. _____
4. _____

Step 7
Homework
Assignment

Changing Yourself

Pick something you do that you would like to change. Pick something simple to start with—like forgetting to do your chores, daydreaming, or biting your nails. Make a plan for how to change that behavior. (Deciding to stop doing something is not enough. Figure out *how* you will stop and who will help you.) Ask someone to help you with your plan. Carry out your plan for one week. Then come back and tell how it went.

My Plan for Change

The thing I do that I want to change: _____

_____

_____

The way I plan to change it:_____

_____

_____

_____

The people who will help me: _____

_____

_____

_____

_____   _____
(Parent/Caretaker Signature)   (Date)

The Step that I learned last week said (write down your answer or have someone else write it for you) _____

_____

_____

_____

_____

I practiced what I learned last week by _____

_____

_____

_____

_____

**STEP
7**

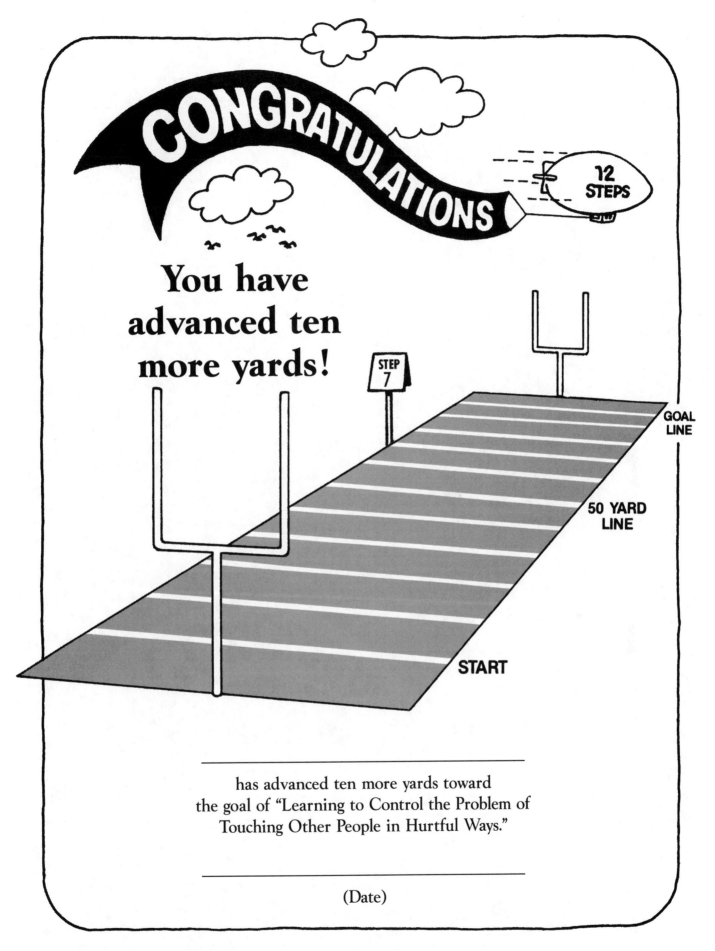

CONGRATULATIONS

12 STEPS

You have advanced ten more yards!

STEP 7

GOAL LINE

50 YARD LINE

START

_____

has advanced ten more yards toward
the goal of "Learning to Control the Problem of
Touching Other People in Hurtful Ways."

_____

(Date)

"I accept that I cannot change other people or their behavior. They are the only ones who can change themselves—and only if they want to. This includes my parents, other grown-ups, and my friends."

STEP
8

Read Step 8 out loud two times slowly.

Things That Bug Me

Make a list of the things about others that really bug you.

Names of people:

1._____

_____

_____

_____

2._____

_____

_____

_____

3._____

_____

_____

4._____

_____

_____

Things that I would like them to change:

1._____

_____

_____

_____

2._____

_____

_____

_____

3._____

_____

_____

4._____

_____

_____

Remember, you cannot change other people. What things can you say to yourself to accept that you can't change others and that you are not responsible for them? Practice saying these things out loud to yourself.

Now look at your list of things people do that really bug you. Make a list on this page of things that you could say to yourself about each of those "buggy" things. Remember, you can *ask* people to change, but you can't *make* them change. You *can* help yourself feel less bugged.

1. _____

_____

_____

2. _____

_____

_____

3. _____

_____

_____

4. _____

_____

_____

P.S. Many of the things that bug us the most are pretty small. So, a good motto to remember is "Don't Sweat the Small Stuff!"

Step 8
Homework
Assignment

Make a list of one thing that you like about each member of your family (including yourself) and one thing that you wish was different. Put a check mark next to the things you think you can change. Put a zero next to the things that only they can change. Show your list to your family, if you feel like it.

Person's Name	Something I Like About Them

Step 8
Homework
Assignment

Something I Wish Was Different	Who Can Change It

_____   _____
(Parent/Caretaker Signature)   (Date)

The Step that I learned last week said (write down your answer or have someone else write it for you) _____

_____

_____

_____

_____

I practiced what I learned last week by _____

_____

_____

_____

_____

STEP
8

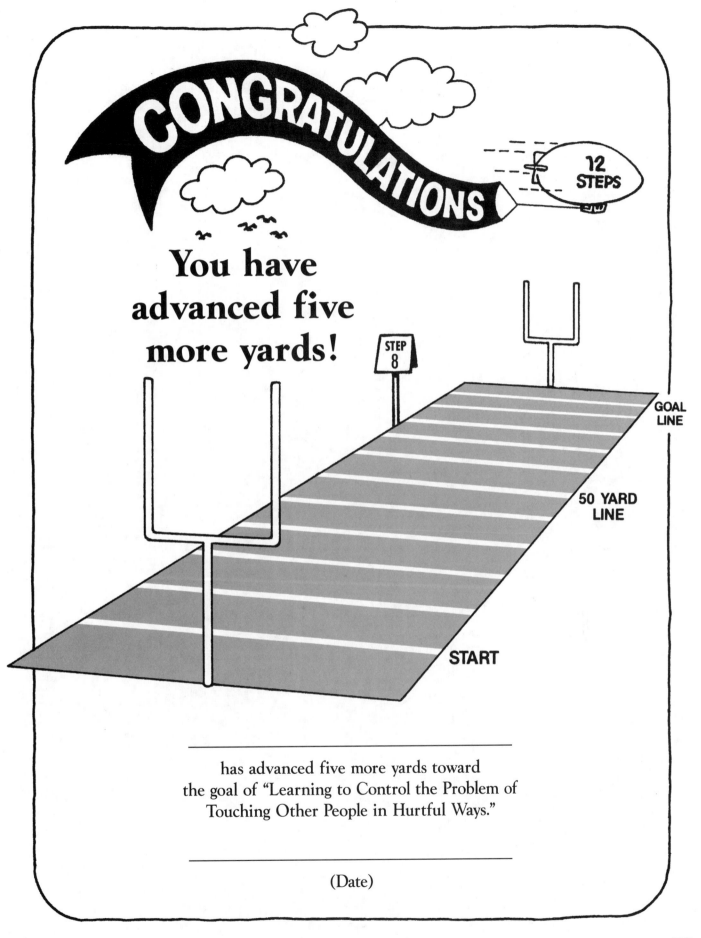

CONGRATULATIONS

12 STEPS

You have advanced five more yards!

STEP 8

GOAL LINE

50 YARD LINE

START

_____

has advanced five more yards toward
the goal of "Learning to Control the Problem of
Touching Other People in Hurtful Ways."

_____

(Date)

"I am learning to recognize the times when I need help from others, including God, and I am willing to ask for help because I need it."

STEP 9

Read Step 9 out loud two times slowly.

"I am learning to recognize the times when I need help from others, and I am willing to ask for help because I need it."

ALTERNATIVE
STEP
9

Read Step 9 out loud two times slowly.

Make a list or write a description of the different times lately that you've asked for help. Who did you ask?

HELP!

_____

_____

_____

_____

_____

Draw a picture of you asking for help.

Make a list of some things you think you might need help with in the future.

1. _____

_____

_____

2. _____

_____

_____

3. _____

_____

_____

4. _____

_____

_____

5. _____

_____

_____

6. _____

_____

_____

My Danger Signs

Our bodies and our minds have ways of telling us when something is wrong or when we're feeling certain things. For example, getting goose bumps on your skin when you're cold, getting a knot in your stomach when you're nervous, or having a nightmare after you've seen a scary movie are all messages from your body or your mind that tell you how you're feeling. They are called "danger signs" because they warn you that there will be trouble ahead if you don't pay attention to them and get help.

Think about the feeling, thinking, and body messages that will let you know that you might be in danger of touching someone again in ways that are wrong. Can you remember any danger signs, thoughts, or body messages that you had just before you touched someone the last time?

Now think about the *feelings* you might get that would make you want to touch someone again in a way that is wrong. Write down these feelings so that you will not forget them.

My Danger Sign Feelings

_____

_____

_____

_____

_____

(Remember, it's okay to have feelings. It's not okay to touch in hurtful ways just because you have certain feelings. You can do other things with your feelings.)

My Body
Messages

Sometimes our bodies give us messages or warning signs that tell us we're upset or that we may be heading for trouble. Think about the signs your body gives you when you're thinking about touching. Mark them on the drawing. Then talk about them.

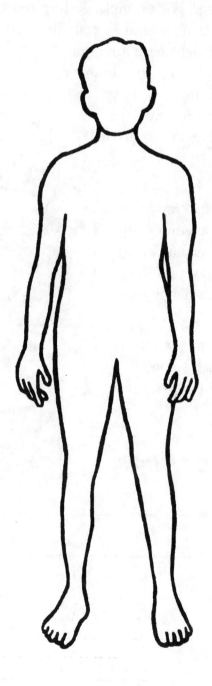

What can you do if your body gives you messages that it wants to touch or be touched in ways that are wrong? One thing you can do is physical exercise—like running or riding your bike. What else could you do? How about asking someone to help you control those body feelings? Who will you ask?

Danger
Sign
Thoughts

There are times when you might start thinking about what you did or what you might do again if you have the chance. Picturing it in your mind might even get you turned on or excited. Those kinds of thoughts (which some people call "fantasies") are danger sign thoughts and they should tell you that you need to talk to someone and ask for help right away.

Danger sign thoughts can lead to bad messages you say to yourself. Remember the vulture who criticizes you? This is like another vulture in your head that says negative things about your touching problem. Things like, "I don't care if I get in trouble or hurt someone else, I want to do it anyway." Write down some dangerous things that you or your vulture might say to you when you're having these kinds of thoughts.

Vulture Talk

1. " _____

   _____

   _____ "

2. " _____

   _____

   _____ "

3. " _____

   _____

   _____ "

You know how to talk back to that vulture. You learned how in Step 6. You can tell it to stop, you can tell it that it's wrong, and you can make those bad thoughts and messages go away. Write down the things you will say to that vulture and to yourself that will help the danger sign thoughts disappear.

Vulture Back-Talk

1. "_____

_____

_____"

2. "_____

_____

_____"

3. "_____

_____

_____"

4. "_____

_____

_____"

Dangerous Situations

Certain situations also can be dangerous for kids who are trying to control their problem with touching. Situations are dangerous if they can make it harder for you to control your touching. Some examples of situations that might be dangerous are being left alone with the kid you touched or with someone who reminds you of that kid, being alone when you're angry or upset, or hanging around with older kids who get into trouble or talk a lot about sex.

What kinds of situations do you think could be dangerous for you these days? (Hint: If you say "none," then you have forgotten that your problem is bigger than you are.)

Draw or write down some of the situations that might make it hard for you to control your touching. Use the next page if you need more space to draw.

How can you avoid being in these situations? Who will you ask to help you?

Dangerous Situations

Step 9
Homework
Assignment

During the week, pay attention to when you are upset and find yourself reacting strongly to something, when things are going wrong, when you're getting mad or somebody's mad at you, or when you're really scared or crying or getting into a fight. When it's all over and you're feeling better, sit down and answer these questions:

1. What happened just before you got upset? _____

_____

_____

2. What were your feelings when you started to react? _____

_____

3. Where did you feel it in your body? _____

_____

4. What other signals told you how strongly you were feeling? _____

_____

_____

5. What did you do to calm yourself down afterward? _____

_____

_____

6. How do you feel about it now? _____

_____

_____   _____
(Parent/Caretaker Signature)   (Date)

The Step that I learned last week said (write down your answer or have someone else write it for you)_____

_____

_____

_____

_____

I practiced what I learned last week by _____

_____

_____

_____

_____

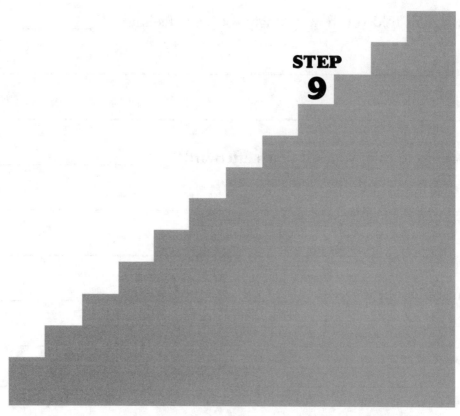

STEP
9

has advanced ten more yards toward
the goal of "Learning to Control the Problem of
Touching Other People in Hurtful Ways."

_____

(Date)

"I have made a list of everyone I have hurt by my behavior (including myself), and I will try to make up, in any way I can, for the harm that I have caused."

STEP 10

Read Step 10 out loud two times slowly.

My Amends List

Think about all of the people you've hurt with your touching problem. Make a list of the people you've hurt, and try to think of a way to make up for the hurt. Some people call this "making amends."

Who I've hurt:

1. _____

2. _____

3. _____

4. _____

5. _____

How I've hurt them:

1. _____

2. _____

3. _____

4. _____

5. _____

How I'd like to make up for the hurt:

1. _____

2. _____

3. _____

4. _____

5. _____

It is not always possible to make up for what you did to some people. It may not be possible to have any contact with them. When that is the situation, what kinds of things could you do instead?

Maybe you could prepare yourself to do something in case you ever get the chance when you're older. Maybe you can do something for someone else instead. Maybe you can work very hard on controlling your problem so that you won't have to make amends to anyone else.

What else could you do? Draw or write it here.

Step 10
Homework
Assignment

Remember a time when you did something mean to someone else, did something dishonest like lying or stealing, or when you hurt somebody's feelings (even if you didn't mean to do it). It doesn't matter how long ago it was or whether they still remember it. Now, figure out a way to "make amends" to that person and do it this week. For example, you could go and tell them you're sorry for what you did, or you could write them a letter. If they don't remember what happened, you should remind them of what you know you did, even if they didn't know about it.

Step 10
Homework
Assignment

My Amend

1. What I did that I needed to apologize for: _____

_____

_____

_____

2. Who I made my amend to: _____

_____

3. What I did or said: _____

_____

_____

_____

4. How I was feeling when I made my amend: _____

_____

_____

5. The way I feel now that it's over: _____

_____

_____

_____

_____   _____
(Parent/Caretaker Signature)   (Date)

The Step that I learned last week said (write down your answer or have someone else write it for you) _____

_____

_____

_____

_____

_____

I practiced what I learned last week by _____

_____

_____

_____

_____

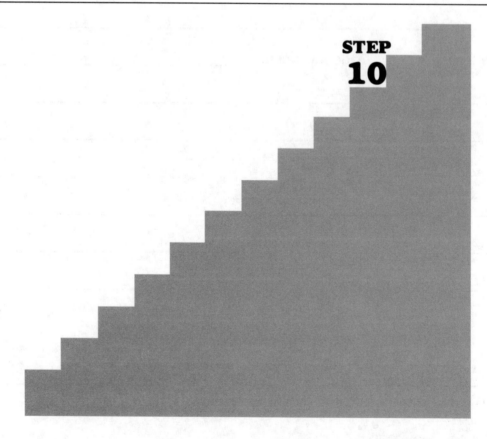

STEP 10

has advanced five more yards toward
the goal of "Learning to Control the Problem of
Touching Other People in Hurtful Ways."

(Date)

"I continue to think about my problem, and I am willing to ask for help if I feel it coming back."

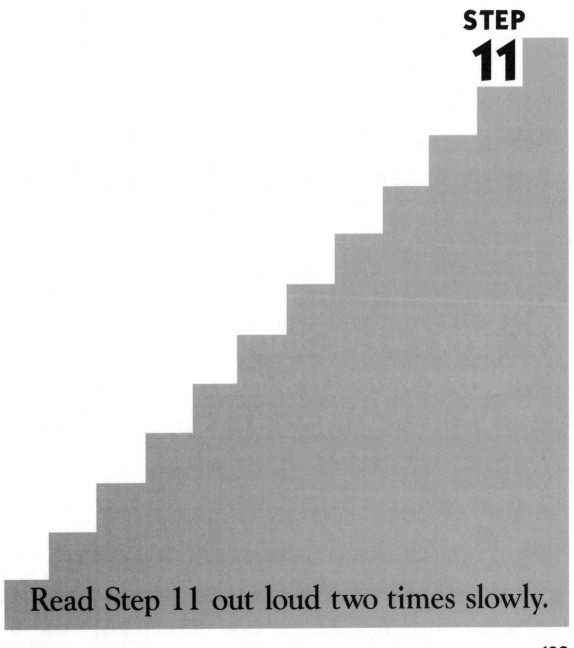

**STEP
11**

Read Step 11 out loud two times slowly.

My
Danger
Signs

It is very important to remember your danger signs.
Write them or draw them on this page.

My danger signs:

Thinking . . .

Feeling . . .

Doing . . .

Situations . . .

How I will ask for help:

When you feel your danger signs coming back, what things will you do?
Write them here.

DANGER

1. _____

_____

_____

2. _____

_____

_____

3. _____

_____

_____

4. _____

_____

_____

5. _____

_____

_____

Step 11
Homework
Assignment

Take time to stop and think about your touching problem at least once this week. Think about all the things you've said and heard about it as you have worked through the steps. Write down what you are thinking or saying to yourself about your problem now. Here are some sentences to fill in to get you started.

1. I still think that my touching problem is _____

_____

2. When I think about my problem I feel _____

_____

3. I think I did it because _____

_____

4. I think therapy is _____

_____

5. I think I am _____

_____

6. Other thoughts I have about my problem: _____

_____

_____

_____

_____

Step 11
Homework
Assignment

Now write down at least three things you have learned about your problem since you started therapy.

1. _____

_____

_____

_____

_____

2. _____

_____

_____

_____

_____

3. _____

_____

_____

_____

_____

_____   _____
(Parent/Caretaker Signature)   (Date)

The Step that I learned last week said (write down your answer or have someone else write it for you) _____

_____

_____

_____

_____

I practiced what I learned last week by _____

_____

_____

_____

_____

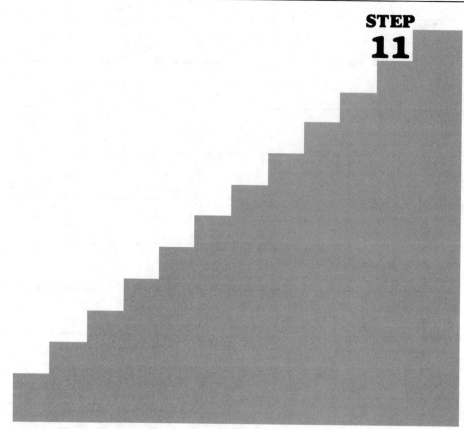

STEP
11

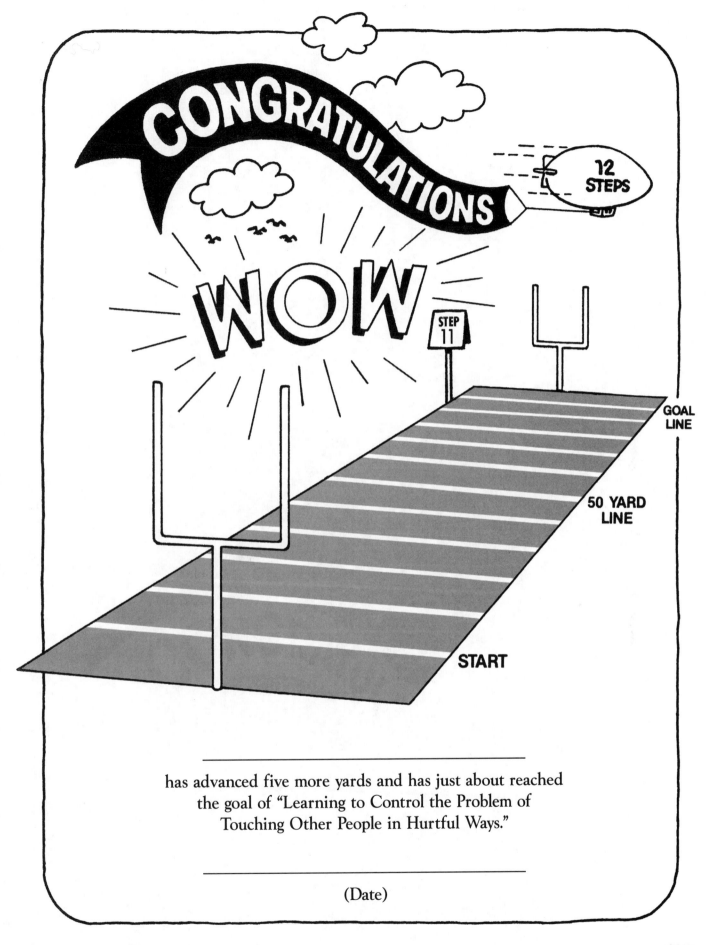

has advanced five more yards and has just about reached
the goal of "Learning to Control the Problem of
Touching Other People in Hurtful Ways."

_____

(Date)

"I will help other kids who have this problem by sharing my own problem and feelings and by helping them to see that it is too tough to handle by themselves."

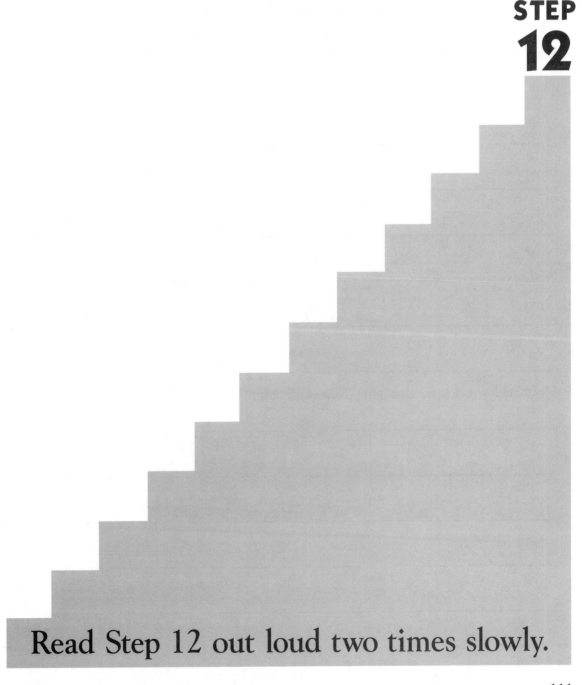

STEP

12

Read Step 12 out loud two times slowly.

Make a list of the ways you might be able to help other kids who have this touching problem.

1. _____

_____

_____

2. _____

_____

_____

3. _____

_____

_____

4. _____

_____

_____

How will you know that they have a problem?

_____

_____

_____

_____

Draw yourself sharing and helping other kids with the same problem.

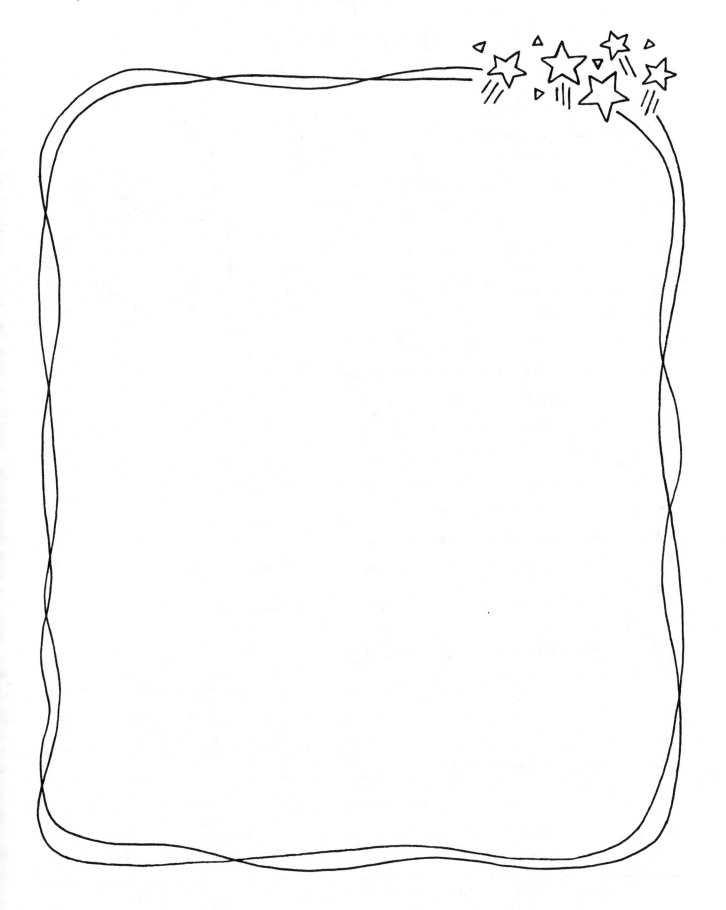

Step 12
Homework
Assignment

A person who helps someone else just for the joy of helping is sometimes called a "good samaritan." Your assignment is to try being a good samaritan for a day.

Think of someone you know or find a situation where there is someone who could use your help. It could be a member of your family, a friend, a neighbor, a person with a disability, or a kid you don't even know. Think of something helpful you could do for that person and then ask if he or she would like your help. If the answer is "no," find someone else to help.

Some examples of helpful things you might do are

- ▼ Help your brothers or sisters (or parents) with their chores
- ▼ Help your teacher after school
- ▼ Cheer up someone who is sad or upset
- ▼ Help someone with his or her homework
- ▼ Help to stop a fight from happening
- ▼ Call or visit someone who is sick
- ▼ Teach someone something that you do well
- ▼ Bonus points: Tell people how much you appreciate them

What are some other helpful things you could do?

Good Samaritan for a Day

1. The name of the person(s) I helped: _____

2. What I did: _____

_____

3. The way I felt afterward: _____

_____

_____

_____
(Parent/Caretaker Signature)   _____
(Date)

The Step that I learned last week said (write down your answer or have someone else write it for you) _____

_____

_____

_____

_____

I practiced what I learned last week by _____

_____

_____

_____

_____

STEP
12

Lessons
Learned

If you have completed all the steps, you have worked hard on your problem with touching. The twelve steps are here to help you learn about yourself and your problem. Here are a few of the things we hope you learned.

Put a ✔ next to the things you know you have learned about yourself.

Put an ✘ next to the things you're not so sure about.

1. _____   Your problem is too tough for you to handle by yourself—but it's not too tough to handle if you get help. You *can* control what you do, and other people can help.

2. _____   You know how to ask for help, and you know who the people are who will help you. All you need to do is ask.

3. _____   You can help yourself, too. You can show your honest feelings to people who can help you handle them—especially when you are upset. You also can use self-talk to make yourself feel better. You even know how to talk back to your "vulture voice" when it gives you negative messages that could get you in trouble.

4. _____   Everyone makes mistakes sometimes—including you. You don't need to blame other people for things that are really your fault. You can admit when you do something wrong. You can even learn important lessons from your mistakes.

5. _____   You can change yourself but not other people. It is their problem to change themselves. You can change some things about yourself—especially your problem with touching—but you cannot change other things. You can learn to accept those things.

6. _____ Good people sometimes do bad things. You are not a bad person just because you do some things that are wrong. The people who love you still love you, even if they hate what you did. You can still love yourself, too.

7. _____ You are learning to think about other people's feelings and how to put yourself in someone else's shoes. You know that what you did wasn't wrong just because you got in trouble—it's wrong because it could be hurtful to other people and because you didn't think about their feelings or how it could affect them.

8. _____ You know that your body and your mind have danger signs that can tell you when something is wrong or when you're feeling certain things. You know you should pay attention to them so that you can ask for help *before* you do something wrong.

9. _____ Your problem is not gone just because you understand it better. You need to stay on the lookout for it and for the feelings that go with it so that you're ready to stop them. If you start to think that you are safe and that you do not have a problem anymore, that's when it could sneak up on you.

10. _____ You know the difference between good touching and bad touching for kids, and you know that you still have to be careful about who you touch and how you touch. You can control your urge to touch in ways that are wrong, but you can still enjoy good touching. You can do that because you want to and because you know that there are lots of people who will help you. They know that you are a special person.

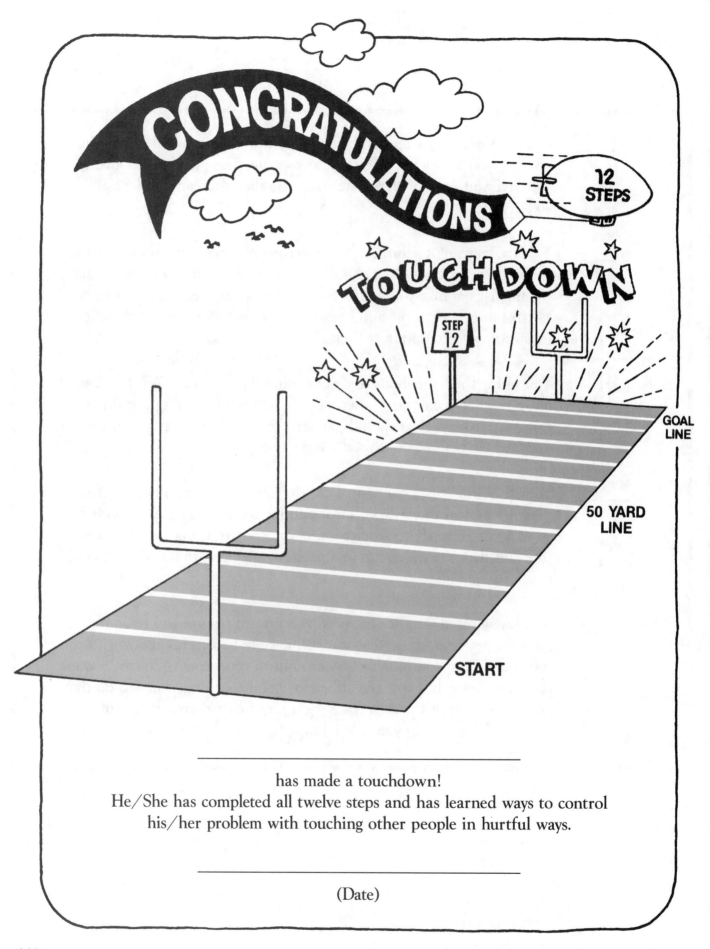

_____

has made a touchdown!
He/She has completed all twelve steps and has learned ways to control
his/her problem with touching other people in hurtful ways.

_____

(Date)

Happy Health

You've made it through the twelve steps. Be proud of yourself! You are on the road to recovery. You are becoming stronger and healthier day by day. Draw a picture of something happy on this last page and ask for a hug from the person or people who helped you complete this workbook.